Liz Byrski is the autho[...] novels including, *Gan[...] Chance Café* and a n[...] books including the popular memoir *Remember Me*. She has worked as a freelance journalist, a broadcaster with ABC Radio and an advisor to a minister in the West Australian Government.

Liz has a PhD from Curtin University where she lectures in creative and professional writing.

www.lizbyrski.com

Also by the Author

Last Chance Café
Bad Behaviour
Trip of a Lifetime
Belly Dancing for Beginners
Food, Sex and Money
Gang of Four

Getting On

Liz Byrski

First published by Momentum in 2012

This edition published in 2012 by Momentum

Pan Macmillan Australia Pty Ltd

1 Market Street, Sydney 2000

A CIP record for this book is available at the National Library of Australia

Getting On: Some Thoughts on Women and Ageing

EPUB format: 9781743340479

Mobi format: 9781743340486

POD format: 9781760081324

Cover design by Red Crayon

Edited by Jo Jarrah

Proofreading by Rosemary Peers

Macmillan Digital Australia: www.macmillandigital.com.au

To report a typographical error, please email
errors@momentumbooks.com.au

Visit www.momentumbooks.com.au to read more about all our books and to buy books online. You will also find features, author interviews and news of any author events.

*For my family and
friends who will occupy
the lighted rooms of my
old age.*

I

Women and the Double Standard of Ageing

> The double standard about aging shows up most brutally in the conventions of sexual feeling, which presuppose a disparity between men and women that operates permanently to women's disadvantage.
>
> — *Susan Sontag*

I have always wanted to be old. Weird? Probably – and certainly neither cool nor fashionable; for that I would need to be a Grumpy Old Woman, whingeing because things aren't what they used to be, and confirming all the assumptions about old women as discontented, obsessed with trivia and generally off their trolleys. And I would need to engage in the 'fight against ageing' to make myself look twenty years younger. But I'm happy to look the age I am, happy

Liz Byrski

to be the age I am. I want to enjoy it, strip-mine it for all it has to offer. I want to live and work with it, not fight it.

But we live in a society in denial about ageing; a denial fuelled by an obsession with image and style, with youth and physical beauty, and the illusion that we can keep making ourselves over to hold old age at bay. And although we are not all obsessed with the desire to stay young, resistance is frequently interpreted as deviance or fail-ure. But there is nothing shameful about ageing; it comes to us all if we are lucky enough to be here to greet it and to deny our age is to pretend to be less than we are in much more than just years.

When I look in the mirror I can see my ageing in the lines, the sagging skin, the ex-tra rolls of fat, the age spots. I can also feel it in my muscles and my joints, the effort of my breath at exercise, the loss of the ability to sit cross-legged, the fact that I have four pairs of glasses but frequently can't find any of them, and that I occasionally discover my misplaced wallet packed in the fridge with the shopping. I creak and puff, I droop and sag. I have given up shoes with heels and the effort to hold in my stomach, and I am working hard on not caring about how I

2

appear to others (although the latter is still a work in progress).

But I can also feel it in my head and in my heart; in my joy in life, my greater appreciation of the world and particularly of my family and friends, my increasing satisfaction in small things, in my waning tolerance of the superficial rhetoric of politicians and the dominant culture of personality and celebrity, which has replaced the culture of character. I see it in disturbing flashes of my own mortality: a glimpse of myself dying alone or the prospect of a long and painful decline, a sharper fear of and greater fascination about the possibilities of an afterlife. I question whether simple aches and pains, lumps and bumps, foreshadow something more serious, even fatal.

I feel my age through my need to make the most of every moment and every day, love more and better, write more and better, learn more, read more. I value family and friends more and more thoughtfully, feel grief more sharply and outrage more passionately. And I relish my age in the pure wonder of having arrived here, two years from seventy, and to be living every day as a bonus and an adventure.

In 1972 the late Susan Sontag suggested that ageing is largely a trial of the imagination. She believed that the anxiety and depression many women experience about ageing is caused by 'the way this society limits how women feel free to imagine themselves'. In that same year Simone de Beauvoir described ageing as 'a class struggle, which, like race and gender, becomes a filter through which to see and understand differential life changes.' Both Sontag and de Beauvoir wrote of the 'double-standard of ageing' – the poisonous nexus of sexism and ageism that disempowers women as they age. We are most desirable as lovers, partners and mothers in our youth, and as that youth fades so too does our sexual value. 'For most women,' Sontag wrote, 'ageing means a gradual process of sexual disqualification.'

Even if, as ageing women, we don't give a damn about sexual disqualification at a personal level it still affects us in both overt and subtle ways. Despite the changes that emerged from the women's movement of the late sixties and seventies we still live in a world predominantly ordained by men, in which the male view of women dictates the visual and verbal wallpaper of our lives.

And it's a particular type of male heterosexuality that defines the overbearing messages about women's value and where it lies. This is not an attack on men; not for one moment do I think that most men are aware of it or even give it a thought, and I know many who do find it as alienating as do many women. But sadly the old bog standard attitudes that defined women's value in terms of their appearance seems to be enjoying a resurgence in the twenty-first century, and it infiltrates the lives of us older, disqualified, women as well as those of younger women and distressingly the lives of little girls.

Is there ever a time in a woman's life when it is okay to be and to look the age she is? Tiny tots are being trained with beauty pageants, pole dancing and Playboy Bunny outfits to mimic the appearance and the sexual appeal of adult women. Girls in their teens strive to appear older until sometime in their twenties, when relentless anti-ageing messages infiltrate their consciousness and they begin to look fearfully over their shoulders. By the thirties middle age is a threat, the fifties and beyond unthinkable. Sexism defines youthful beauty and sexual availability as what matters for women. And so advertisements for fashion, lingerie and cosmetics targeting women are all designed with words and images that play to men's fantasies about women to encourage us to spend in ways that will satisfy those fantasies, until the time we become irrelevant.

It is the end of fertility that marks us out as sexually unattractive and undesirable, and it brings with it the additional assumption that we are moody, depressed and emotionally unstable. But while some women do suffer severe physical and emotional difficulties at menopause, for most the effects are just mild and annoying, and some experience very few symptoms at all. Menopause is the culture's defining consciousness about older women and within it there are several narratives of the 'problem'. There is the medical-problem-medical-solutions story, which treats it as an illness and is accompanied with lists of enough grim physical and psychological symptoms as to make you slash your wrists. It is heavily weighted towards hormone replacement therapy and frequently has a critical edge that implies that while menopause is a clinical condition requiring medical intervention, the woman is selfish and pathetic for seeking help to manage her symptoms. There is the pull-yourself-together-so-you-don't-frighten-the-children-or-upset-the-men story, which counsels women not to bore and embarrass others with this life-changing experience – 'just grin and bear it, and keep taking the tablets'. And finally there is the I-did-it-my-way-with-the-help-of-the-goddess-and-a-few-archetypes; this version is dreamy and mystical and often involves herbs, visualisation and rituals with shells and candles.

All these narratives create the context for menopause as a major design fault that leads inevitability to diminishment, alienation and invisibility. The impact of hormonal change is physiologically and emotionally real, but it is not necessarily debilitating or disabling; even so, biological determinism – used to declare women mad, sad or bad as adolescents and in pregnancy – has a special bite in old age where it also erases us from public view. How can mature women begin to imagine themselves pre, during and after menopause without images of vibrant, content, energetic older women with their own very special beauty.

The imaginative freedom to enjoy ageing, to recognise its possibilities and rise to its challenges, depends to a considerable extent upon how we see it represented in the world around us. Writer and anthropologist Thomas De Zengotita suggests that seeing ourselves and our lives reflected in the products of popular culture is a pervasive and fundamental form of flattery: 'The flattered self is a mediated self,' he writes, 'and the alchemy of mediation is the osmotic process through which reality and representation fuse, and get carried to our psyches by the irresistible flattery that goes with being incessantly addressed.' In other words when we can constantly see realistic representations of people like us in the media we feel we are being acknowledged, spoken to by the creators of those images, included as part of the audience and therefore part of the larger tribe.

But ageing and old women are rarely the central characters in the products of popular culture. They appear in minor stereotypical and frequently negative roles: nosey neighbours, interfering mothers-in-law, dippy old aunts, scheming bitches or frail old burdens who impede the lives and the desires of the really important characters – men, younger women and children. Television, at the heart of most Australian homes, is the place where we should reasonably expect to experience the benefits of representational flattery, but for older women it is a representational void. For ageing women invisibility is both a feeling and reality, and the silence of not being addressed is deafening.

Realistic fictional representations are, I believe, even more powerful in terms of representational flattery than real-life examples of successful women. In the long history of efforts to raise the status of women the existence and visibility of real-life female leaders as role models has always been inspirational, but famous, high-profile women can also seem remote from our own more ordinary lives. It is in fiction – in books and on the screen – that we can experience the inner lives of others, observe their challenges, learn how they deal with anger, grief and loss as well as success, joy, love and fulfilment. In fiction we are privy to the emotional rollercoaster of ordinary lives that reflect our own and in its multiple possibilities we see who we are and who we can become. It works to humanise and to bond us with those who are living with or have already passed through what we have yet to experience.

It was the absence of interesting and realistic older women as the central characters in Australian women's fiction that led me, ten years ago, to start writing novels that feature these characters. I had been searching the shelves of libraries and bookshops for novels that featured women of fifty plus; I wanted to read about women like me. I was in my late fifties then, and surrounded by friends and colleagues of a similar age and older who were living dynamic, useful and rewarding lives. They were, and still are, starting new businesses, enrolling at university, playing the stock market, surfing the waves and the internet, travelling, retraining and falling in and out of love. I regularly interviewed ageing women who held powerful positions in government and business, who excelled in the sciences, the arts and in sport, who had raised money to fund women's scholarships, overseas orphanages, or support services for women and children in crisis. They were doing all this in spite of, as well as, and way beyond menopause. It seemed to me that these women's stories were just as worth telling in fiction and drama as the stories of young women setting out in pursuit of careers and Mr Right offered by chick-lit and rom-coms.

Quite a few people laughed when I spoke of writing novels about older women; quite a few more, particularly those in the media, sucked in their breath, shook their heads, and told me unequivocally that no one would want to read about older women. As women over forty-five buy more books than any other demographic this seemed a frankly stupid assumption and further illustrated the insidious effects of the double standard of ageing. Now, six best-selling novels later, I am delighted to have proved them wrong, but despite this demonstrated market, creators, producers, editors and publishers of popular culture still seem locked into the frantic pursuit of a youthful audience.

My argument is not with young people themselves, many of whom are concerned about and alienated by the sexualisation of marketing in so many areas, and by the pressure to conform to standards of physical beauty and sexual allure which they find unrealistic, undesirable and frequently offensive. Young women and men are profoundly affected by the absence of realistic, interesting and positive stories, images and messages about older people. When young people don't see realistic representations of the rich, diverse and satisfying lives of older people, they cannot see the future possibilities and choices open to them. In my conversations and correspondence with women of all ages and in a variety of contexts the invisibility of older women always rears its head. It's not surprising that many fear age and are drawn into the myth of some sort of battle against it when they cannot see the pleasures, rewards and opportunities that ageing can offer.

If you aren't aware of the double standard of ageing and feel that as a woman you haven't experienced it I urge you to think again, and to look beyond yourself. Wake up to the bigger picture, study the patterns on the wallpaper and listen for the tone of the background music.

II

Invisible Women

> If we do not know what we are going to be we cannot know what we are: let us recognise ourselves in that old man or that old woman. It must be done if we are to take upon ourselves the entirety of our human state.
> — *Simone de Beauvoir*

Each time I walk into a shopping centre or open a women's magazine I wonder if the centre and store managers, the creative directors of advertising and marketing or the editors ever stop to take a look at their customers and their readers, because there is a yawning black hole of disconnection between their imagery and reality. Time was when I could look around and see images of women like me; they were usually thinner, more attractive and more glamorous but it was obvious we were of the same species. On the billboards, the hoardings, the magazine fashion and beauty specials, in advertisements for a whole range of products there were women with whom I could identify. Now, despite our very real physical presence in numbers too big to ignore, women of my age have been erased from public visual space and are surrounded by images and messages that tell us that to be a woman is to be young, slim, beautiful and sexually available. Teenage girls, dazzling in their photoshopped and airbrushed perfection, many of them barely past pubescence, dominate the visual fashion and beauty displays; posing, pouting and selling 'the look' – glossy, sexy, seductive; an unsettling mix of innocence and 'up for it'. Even the advertisements for 'anti-ageing' products target women in their twenties and thirties. And many of the magazines, of which we have been loyal readers for years, confine us to the ghettoes of special sections for the mother (or grandmother) of the bride or detailed advice about cosmetic surgery and other 'weapons' in the fight against ageing. The only aged women on show seem to be movie stars whose faces are eerily plumped with Botox or sculpted by surgery, and whose wrinkles and age spots have been erased by the wonders of photographic software.

In the late decades of the nineteenth century the development of the great department stores, and the magazines that followed in their wake, created for the first time a public space for women. Since those early days women have been targeted by generations of advertising and marketing, encouraging us to view shopping not simply as an element of domestic work, but as pleasure and leisure; to see department stores and shopping centres as our territory, and magazines as a way of understanding our own lives. The twentieth century saw the birth of generations of women encouraged to believe that they were born to shop, to feel at home in stores and malls, and to identify with the women in the pages of the magazines. But now as we age we find ourselves expunged from these familiar, once reassuring, places and publications.

In this cultural climate it's hardly surprising that anxiety about ageing drives women through the revolving door of makeover to undergo cosmetic surgery or other invasive procedures. Some will emerge scarred, burned or freakish, many will end up with faces that are plumped and bloated, stretched to distortion or unnaturally smooth and expressionless. Fighting age extracts a high price psychologically, physically and financially, and its promise is dangerously seductive. The makeover trip from 'before' to 'after' is one in which 'after' immediately transforms into the next 'before'. It is nourished by television programs such as *What Not to Wear*, *How to Look Good Naked* and *Ten Years Younger in Ten Days*. These programs target women at their most vulnerable; frequently overworked and exhausted and often on very tight budgets. Most victims are aged from their late thirties through to their late fifties, on the cusp of middle age or ageing, concerned about their appearance and the threat of menopause and post-menopause. Women past sixty are, clearly, beyond redemption as far as these programs are concerned, and while in some ways that is cause for celebration, it also speaks to the idea that old age is too hideous to contemplate and ageing women are therefore irrelevant.

I first watched Trinny Woodall and Susannah Constantine in *What Not to Wear* with a mounting sense of horror. I remember girls like that from my school days, bossy and sharp-tongued. They were often prefects, house captains or sports captains and seemed to take pleasure in humiliating lesser mortals – younger girls, overweight girls, others plagued with spots and, worst of all, those with bad hair and scruffy uniforms whose mothers forced them to wear socks and sandals or brogues, instead of stockings and pointy shoes with kitten heels. They were adept at sneering and pinching, and they maintained a scathing commentary on the appearance and behaviour of those unfortunate enough to attract their attention.

Woodall and Constantine are much more than just fashion police, they are image and lifestyle terrorists let loose to sneer and curl their lips on television. With extraordinary insensitivity they discuss their victims in the most offensive terms, watch them shop while whispering disparaging asides and grimacing to the camera, and then deliver insulting judgements face to face, frequently reducing the women to tears. Words are then followed by action; they pinch rolls of fat, grab sagging breasts and force them into punishing bras, cram love handles, buttocks and thighs into torturous, more constricting corsetry than their great-grandmothers would have worn.

More user friendly and with a much more positive line of commentary, the eccentric Gok Wan in *How to Look Good Naked* claims to make women love their bodies. He persuades them to strip off in a room full of their peers and compare themselves with others who are larger, smaller, firmer or flabbier. A chosen few are then photographed and their naked images posted on huge hoardings or billboards while onlookers are encouraged to comment on the attractiveness or otherwise of their body parts. Interestingly all this body love seems to apply only to the naked body. When it's time to get dressed for a date, out comes the corsetry, and the pushing, squeezing and hoisting begins. The effort required to disguise the reality of the bodies the women have learned to love (or not) is time consuming, uncomfortable and humiliating. And if this sort of humiliation is not enough, there is always *Ten Years Younger in Ten Days*, in which the victim of the fight against ageing stands inside a glass or perspex box in a public place while confused passers-by are asked to guess their age. In the next equally humiliating and emotionally distressing stage, the victim must watch and listen to the brutal and insulting vox pops before being handed over to a team of 'professionals' who will torture them from head to toe, squeezing, stretching, shaving, injecting, tweezing, and forcing them into brutal exercise regimes to meet the ten-day deadline.

These programs and their clones all sell the idea that we can be made over, made better, slimmer, prettier, sexier and – most important of all – younger. Signs of age can be banished in a minute, an hour, a week, ten days or whatever suits the TV schedules. And if you can't get it done on television with millions watching your prolonged humiliation and fleeting triumph, you can pop into a salon or a clinic near you. Makeover's focus is the moment of the 'reveal' when the victim is at last permitted to see her reflection, and her family, friends and the viewing public gain sight of the finished product. The toxic voyeurism of makeover ignores the past and cuts off the future; it tramples over the whole person and their inner life to create a product with a very short shelf-life. In the case of the hair and makeup, which are so crucial to the 'reveal', this may just be a matter of hours. The corsetry will soon be abandoned on the grounds of pain, discomfort, overheating or the humiliation of being seen in such hideous gear by a lover. And within a few months the distorted plasticity of the injections, the sag and pull of the stretching, cutting and stitching will reveal the need for regular and expensive maintenance. The aggressively promoted fight against ageing is not a fight which can be won, and its lie consumes women's time, energy and self-esteem, chipping away at the inner sense of self.

One of the complaints of seventies feminism was that the pressure on women to achieve and maintain culturally approved and expected standards of feminine appearance diverted their energy, time and money away from other, more interesting, valuable and empowering goals – such as educational, professional and creative development. It trained them for compliance and set them up to be judged on their physical and facial beauty or lack of it in every area of their lives. The women's movement created considerable attitudinal change in this area but that progress has now been trashed by the market-driven concept of post-feminism, in which a woman's worth is tied to even more crippling standards of beauty and style than in earlier decades. Post-feminism, an invention of the neo-liberalism of the late eighties, has kidnapped the language and the tropes of feminism and turned it against women in the form of a multi-million dollar industry of image makeover. Feminism fought the focus on women's appearance on the grounds that women were worth so much more. Now the image industries have reduced our worth to anti-ageing creams and mascara wands, because 'you're worth it'. When youth, beauty and sex appeal are all that matters, the fear of their decline hovers threateningly over the shoulders of young and old alike.

Small wonder then that as the years slip by many ageing women will succumb to the pressure of makeover and attempt to pass as younger. But age passing is a dangerous game in which the player is perched on the knife-edge of lying, to herself and others. The lie that is required to portray a coherent identity and the vigilance needed to maintain it – undermines the self.

I don't want to cut and paste myself into a history that would make me ten or twenty years younger, nor to submit myself to uncomfortable, painful and invasive techniques that promise to make me something

I am not. My past is precious to me; it is packed with wonderful, funny, generous, wise and brilliant people, and some troublesome, bitter and confused souls too. It is littered with highs and lows, dismal failures and the times I got things right. I don't want to erase any of it in order to pretend I'm ten or fifteen years younger. Why shouldn't I speak of my age and take pride in it?

A woman who embraces her own ageing and rejects the proposition that she should even want to look twenty years younger is viewed at best with curiosity and at worst with distaste. Ageing women whose sense of identity is not dependent on external beauty represent ways of being old that undermine the myth of makeover, and so present a threat to the vested interests that have created this pseudo fight against ageing. As a result they are denied recognition, visibility and cultural relevance.

The double standard of ageing makes us invisible, but while invisibility disempowers, disadvantages and isolates us it also has a more beneficial side – the liberation of not being seen. Girls grow to adulthood in the knowledge that they are looked at and judged by men and by other women, and as women we develop the habit of self-surveillance and an often acute facility for self-criticism and self-deprecation. In youth it seems flattering to be the object of constant attention but as we age we become weary of the price it extracts, the need for constant awareness of how we look, the anxiety around disapproval and of attracting the wrong sort of male attention. The critical male eye appraises us and finds us wanting as, we believe, do the eyes of women younger, more attractive and better dressed than ourselves.

As I shuffle through the school photographs taken in my teens I can see my own self-consciousness and feel once more the sharp edge of remembered envy and unease because the others were all so much prettier, taller and slimmer than me, they had better hair and clothes. The camera captures that self-awareness in the tension of my smile and the way my eyes seem always on the verge of turning away. With the benefit of age I can see the same insecurities in the other faces too, insecurities that I couldn't see back then. I have never possessed the sort of beauty or sex appeal that turns heads; a career as a bikini model was never on the cards and my body has always defied the confines of the most modest swimwear, but in those photographs I can see that when it came to looks there was very little to choose between us. The awareness of scrutiny and the fear of not measuring up as girls or women is there in our faces from a very early age, just as it is present in the overdone smiles, poked out tongues or aggressive grins accompanied by two fingers in the photographs that I see of young women on Facebook.

But old age can release us from this. It is the time when we are free to be as daring or as dowdy as we wish, and to stop worrying about what others think. The pressures and the judgements about the way we look can be a straightjacket. Women are expected to perform being female, by paying attention to our appearance, by constantly checking the mirror for defects, by expecting to be looked at and to respond to that looking. We are encouraged to spend time on ourselves, striving for 'the look' or some version of it and then criticised for being superficial and vain. Age, if we let it, can free us from that tyranny, but those decades of scrutiny and judgement ensure that it takes time and effort to rid ourselves of appearance anxiety. Sometimes I think I may be getting better at not caring, but then I'll find myself slipping back into the old concern about what others might think. In reality, of course, even the fashion police have no interest in how an old woman looks, obsessed as they are by worrying about their own appearance. It is only when our appearance has the power to embarrass a younger person who may be seen with us that they are at all interested in what we wear and how we look.

For a writer the invisibility of age is also licence to watch – even to stare – and to listen. Few people notice an old woman staring at them, and if I have to share a café table with strangers they rarely seem to moderate their conversations. Perhaps they assume I am deaf, or are fooled by the book I carry, but I doubt they give me a second thought, let alone realise that I am listening to speech patterns, accents, cadences and colloquialisms, and the real-life dramas discussed over their cappuccinos. 'All writers are thieves; theft is a necessary tool of the trade,' says the novelist Nina Bawden. A writer's mind is a melting pot of ideas harvested from the stuff of everyday life: from what we experience, what we are told or overhear, what we read, see around us, dream and imagine. From that melting pot of fragments, stories and characters emerge and take on new life in forms and circumstances unrecognisable from their origins. Harvesting is richer when one can do it without being noticed.

Invisibility has its roots in assumptions about old people, about their passivity, their annoying but largely harmless presence, the possibility that they are deaf or daft. But that old double standard that differentiates women from men also subjects us to the idea that the loss of fertility inevitably means the loss of intellectual ability, creativity, vision, manual dexterity and, perhaps most important of all, the loss of any need to freely imagine who and what we want to be at this time of life. Ironically, later life is the time when women are often free to explore and develop new and different ways to be. The multiple facets of invisibility can be convenient and liberating for those confident enough to make the most of it. But the impact of erasing a large percentage of the population from public view dismisses and disempowers those people; it allows the reality of their lives, and their contribution to society to remain hidden and frequently unacknowledged and unrewarded. And it restricts their ability to imagine themselves in different, stimulating and challenging ways.

III

The Personal Is Political

> If we continue to see our
> own age through the eyes of
> observers much younger, we
> will find it impossible to
> understand the peculiar
> satisfactions of being older.
> — *Germaine Greer*

You won't find the slogan 'make age invisible' written into the policies of any
politician or political party, but you can
be sure that hiding the elderly population,
particularly elderly women, is politically
savvy and strategic. By all means talk
about the problem of the ageing population, the costs, the terrifying issues it raises
for the future, make all the right moth-
erhood statements, nod sagely to indicate
you are contemplating solutions, but don't
open up the discussion, because the

invisibility of older women is a can of worms. Shine a light on ageing women and you will be forced to see them and to acknowledge the number of other older and much younger people who are dependent upon or sustained by their unpaid work. Worse still you might be forced to cost that work and publish the figures. Far better to obfuscate and mask the truth of the billions of dollars saved on the care of intellectually and physically disabled adults and children in those old women's own families and communities, on tending the dying in their own homes, caring for both their own and other people's grandchildren, chauffeuring others to hospital and medical appointments, delivering library books and meals on wheels, running the trolley services and cafés in hospitals, collecting and distributing food and clothing to disadvantaged people, and so much more. Hide it or ignore it and you don't have to cost it, admit to it or do anything about it. If ageing and old women went on strike, if they stopped doing all that unpaid and unacknowledged caring, support and sheer hard labour, the country would grind to a halt. Invisibility really does matter at an individual and a collective level.

Not every older woman is aware of invisibility at a personal level but millions more are; they rage against it both silently and overtly and are dispirited and damaged by it. Some men also experience it but men have always had the advantage in the age stakes. It is acceptable for men to grow old, to show their age and to assume that they still have a chance of attracting much younger women.

But despite the frustrations of invisibility and its pernicious effects, despite the inequalities of the double standard of ageing many older women are making the most of ageing. And because women live longer and tend, in age, to be more self-sufficient and involved in the lives of families and communities than are men, we are well placed to enjoy our longevity.

Getting old is real, complex and multifaceted and it is certainly not for wimps, but while I don't want to underestimate the undeniable negatives of loneliness, isolation, ill health, financial hardship, lack of mobility and other realities, I also want to hear about the positives, which are just as real. And I crave a public conversation that does not always frame the ageing population as a problem.

I live in an old outer suburb of Perth and there are a lot of us wrinklies here. Some of my neighbours have lived in this street for more than fifty years. You can't really avoid old people here, we're everywhere, charging off on walks at first light or sunset, watering our gardens, riding our bikes, volunteering, acting as carers of even older people and small children, and having opinions on everything. Some of us even have the cheek to still be working full- or part-time into our seventies. We pollute the tree-lined streets, the shopping centres, the many coffee shops, the footpaths and the parks with our oldness; a constant, unpleasant reminder to younger generations of what lies ahead. We have been problematised; graffitied with dire predictions about unsustainable budget deficits and forthcoming crises in the economy, housing, health and community services. We are, apparently, leaching the lifeblood from the richest younger generations in history by doing just what those younger people also aspire to do – live healthy, active, enriching lives for longer than previous generations. We're a splendid example of the triumph of a first rate health care system, advances in education and technology and the success of a reasonably civil society. Why don't we celebrate all this? Why don't we change the language from problem to achievement, from threat to inspiration and promise? The public discourse on ageing is overwhelmingly negative; it ricochets back and forth between denial, attack and defence, leaving many older people, who worked hard and paid taxes all their lives struggling to understand the apparent resentment of their continued existence.

In this twenty-first century, where makeover culture dominates, ageing people have the new responsibility of achieving a state of agelessness by stretching middle-age or, at the very least, if we absolutely must hang around getting old, adopting a strategy of 'successful ageing' in which we not only look but behave younger than we are. Researcher and writer Meredith Jones explains that this involves attempts to elasticise one's real age by the use of hormone replacement therapies, pharmaceuticals, cosmetic surgery and social activities. And an essential part of this is projecting a youthful image to the world. That image requires evidence of having done the work necessary for 'success', and possibly also having had some work done *on* oneself. You can see it in those tanned, silver-haired, heterosexual couples with good teeth, walking hand-in-hand or arms entwined along the beach in advertisements for superannuation, 55+ lifestyle villages and dietary fibre capsules. The message is that if we work hard and do everything right then we can expect to be happy and popular, enjoy financial security and be loved and admired for ageing successfully. How patronising. The advice comes from 'experts' or at least from their marketing spokespeople who seem unable to grasp the idea that being old might just be another joyful, challenging and intriguing stage of life. Is the fight against ageing a displacement activity for the young and middle-aged who are overwhelmed by fear and loathing of their own ageing?

Many of us from our sixties through to our nineties and beyond are doing more and have higher expectations of ageing and old age than our parents and grandparents did and had, but sixty is not the new forty, nor eighty the new sixty. We know this despite the patronising instructions of those experts and marketers, the politicians and the gurus who profess to have the answers to the 'problem' of ageing. We know it because we feel it, we see it, we experience it every day. Within ourselves we may frequently entertain the illusion that we are somewhere between eighteen and thirty-five – after all, in many ways we do *feel* the same – but at the same time we know who and what we are: we are old, older, ageing or aged. All of that, some of that, whatever! We may still swim, surf, ride bikes, play sudoku, complete complex crosswords and get to grips with new technology, travel the world, fall in love and study for the higher degrees we failed to pursue in our youth, but we both approach and experience all this in different ways from the ways of our youth, and our priorities shift with the passing years.

It makes sense for each of us to approach our own ageing with respect, but the idea of 'successful ageing' is rooted in concepts of control and mastery rather than acceptance and openness to new and different experiences. And its dark side is the pressure to perform ageing to the world in ways that will alleviate younger people's fear, and avoid for ourselves the shame of failure. But the ability to remain physically fit and sexually and romantically active as we age depends on so much more than positive thinking, diet, exercise, top dentistry and the cosmetics industry. We bring to age not just the stories of our lives, but all the baggage of genetic inheritance, health, education, family ties or the lack of them, our savings and superannuation or lack of them, and our various problems of housing and mobility, which may be beyond our individual control. The challenge of 'successful ageing' makes excessive and unrealistic demands on older people and sets up a context for failure.

Try as we might to stay fit and active from middle-age it is usually our bodies that deliver the first reality check and, unlike the pre-war generation, we late war babies and baby boomers have grown up with the expectation that things can be fixed. We assume that medical science, technology, pharmaceuticals and developments in transport and communications can be relied upon to keep us trim, taut and terrific, in touch, vertical and mobile, and to repair us when we start to fall apart. But as we trundle through our fifties and sixties, most of us will face some sort of physical challenge; it's the reality check for which there is no quick-fix prescription. As the doctor shakes her head and talks heart attack, stroke and all the other diseases and conditions of ageing, we will discover to our dismay that the solutions lie in the things we know we should have been doing for the past twenty years or more: losing weight, cutting back on alcohol, taking regular exercise and reducing stress.

My mother, who had been a dancer, thought most forms of sport and organised physical exercise were unsuitable for girls and unladylike. She gave the nod to swimming but was disgusted that I was required to play hockey and netball (almost as disgusted as me), and was always an easy touch for a note to the games mistress to get me out of the agony of running barelegged around a hockey field on freezing afternoons. In later life nothing was more worthy of her contempt than gyms, exercise equipment and team sports. But she certainly understood the need to stay active, and this she achieved by walking her dogs quite long distances every day and encouraging me to walk with her. I loathed games and gyms and remain eternally grateful to her for protecting me from at least some of the horrors of school sports. But it's also convenient for me to blame her for my lifelong resistance to a regular pattern of exercise and physical activity.

As I've grown older concern for future mobility and independence combined with the sudden onset of arthritis in my knees has finally motivated me to take exercise more seriously. And so several times a week I am one of a cluster of elderly people waiting for the doors of the gym to open at seven. It's a special sort of gym though – no shiny lycra, no headbands or bouncy pony tails, no bulked-up blokes grunting as they pump iron. Even the two youthful exercise physiologists eschew the image-conscious style of the large flashy gyms and look like just what they are – friendly, competent professionals doing their job. No disco, no thumping rock, no preening, just the space, the equipment and the expertise needed to get the middle-aged, the elderly and anyone in rehab moving and improving. My previous and fleeting experiences in gyms have been intimidating and alienating. The fixed expressions, the headphones and iPods, the lip gloss and fake tans, the fashion parade of leotards, tights, shorts and leggings and the line-up of flexing biceps, shaved chests and tight buttocks are anathema to the overweight, the faint-hearted and the elderly. I wonder how many older people never get past the threshold of a gym because the glossy, sexy, youth-focused environments make them turn away at the door.

On other days I'm one of a different, larger cluster of people waiting for the doors of the swimming pool to open at 5.30 am and minutes later I'm chest deep in the 25-metre pool where the water is pleasantly close to body temperature and at least 70 percent of the people are my age or older, and 90% are women. We swarm up and down the lanes walking forwards, backwards and sideways, stretching our limbs beyond the limits that constrain us on dry land; it's a magical world in which we are kilos lighter, more flexible, more mobile and more comfortable. Each time I get into the water my joints resist the effort of moving against it, but with the extended stretch of each step I feel I am elongating, as though muscles that cramped and contracted overnight are grasping the challenge of moving freely. When I swim my body remembers how it felt when, as a plump, unathletic teenager with a huge crush on the lifeguard, I struggled to win his approval by swimming a full mile. My arms remember that they can reach further and pull harder, my hips and legs find their own rhythm. Here I am stronger, faster, better, I am practically bionic, at least until I have to stop for breath. The arthritis reality check has helped me to change when I least expected to. It has made me stick with the program long enough to feel the benefit and even to enjoy it.

Compared to many of my contemporaries and much older people, who still compete in the annual 18-kilometre swim from Perth to Rottnest Island, who walk marathons and climb mountains and ride hundreds of kilometres on their bikes each week, my efforts are long overdue and pretty pathetic. But now at least I'm in there, not fighting ageing but working with it, and that feels good. I have no need or desire to look ten or twenty years younger, or to do all the things I did in my thirties and forties. Pushing back time is wasting time. I prefer to embrace ageing, examine it for the ways it can be challenging and different, for the ways I can be different, rather than viewing it as an extended diminishment that has to be tolerated. But, sadly, acceptance, curiosity and discovery are rarely part of the public conversation on ageing.

IV

Facing Age

I have always longed to be old, and that is because all my life I have had such wonderful exemplars of old age, such marvelous models to contemplate.
— *May Sarton*

I was a late war baby, the only child of older parents, and I grew up through the forties and fifties on the edge of a small English village, from where there were just two buses a day to the closest town. My nearest school friend lived twelve miles, three bus changes or a forty-five minute bike ride away; the daughter of a nearby farmer was my first and only accessible friend. I lived in my parents' world and spent a lot of time alone or with their friends, many of whom were elderly. These older people fascinated me; they had wisdom, confidence and the freedom to determine where they went and how they spent their time. I wanted what they had and so perhaps my curiosity about and enthusiasm for ageing is not as surprising as it might, at first, seem.

I can't tell one of those stories of childhood trauma so popular these days because, despite the strange and inexplicable tension between my parents, I had a fortunate and happy childhood. To outsiders we probably seemed a perfect family; charming middle-class couple with bright and dutiful daughter. Well dressed, well fed, well heeled and largely, I think, well liked and respected. But when I reflect now on the atmosphere at home I see that I was so accustomed to tension and anxiety that it had become my normal state. We were a classic triangle and constant attention to mood and tone was needed to maintain equilibrium. My role was clear: do well at school, work hard, behave perfectly at all times, eschew anger in favour of hurt and keep quiet about it, attend to the needs of others before my own. Once you know the rules, and I knew them from a very early age, you have a kind of safety; you believe that if you stick to them everything will be all right. I stuck to those rules way beyond childhood and teens into my twenties and everything *was* all right. I was both happy and content. My parents may not have been able to love each other but they loved me, and they made sure I knew it.

At sixteen I told my parents I wanted to be a writer, and I can still see the dismay on my father's face. Writing, he said, was not a real job, not a reliable way to earn a living. While I would doubtless get married I should also hedge my bets and prepare for life by being able to support myself with a 'proper job', otherwise I could become a burden on the economy. My mother had other concerns; women writers, she said, were bossy, opinionated and interfering and no one would marry me. It didn't strike me then, but now, more than five decades later, it seems a strange view for a woman who loved reading and who, I now believe, lived much of her life through books, predominantly books written by women.

My father was right in that it really is hard to earn a living as a writer, but I have been doing it for most of my life and I haven't yet become a burden on the economy. My mother was both right and wrong. Two people did marry me – not, I hasten to add, at the same time, and they did so *before* I became bossy, opinionated and interfering. But back in 1960, although career prospects for young women were certainly broader and more appealing than at any other time since the war, middle-class girls were encouraged towards something ladylike and respectable that would precede marriage and later – if, God forbid, it proved necessary – be fitted around a family.

My parents did mention the possibility of university, but it was a bit of a mystery to the three of us. No one in our family had ever been to university and while Mum and Dad understood the destinations for graduates with degrees in law or medicine I don't think they had any idea what one might do with a degree in literature or history. And so I was steered, like so many other young women at the time, towards the choice of teacher, nurse or secretary, none of which required a degree in those days. When I tell this to young women today they always ask why I didn't talk to the careers officer at school, and they are amazed to learn that such people didn't exist then. They are even more shocked to learn that you couldn't pop down to the pharmacy to buy a pregnancy testing kit when your period didn't arrive – but that's another story.

I had no desire to care for the sick, and as a solitary only child was terrified by the prospect of being in charge of a class of unruly children. And so I became a bored and inefficient secretary. A few years later, languishing in an airline office at Gatwick Airport, I got to know the Reuters reporter who regularly used my phone to dictate his copy. It dawned on me then that journalism might be a good job for someone who wanted to write so I badgered him for information and contacts, and eventually got my foot in the door of the local newspaper. Once again my poor father was horrified; journalism, he said, involved poking one's nose into other people's business. This, naturally, made the prospect even more attractive to me. But I also remained clear about the need to find a husband and the humiliation that would be mine if I ended up left on the shelf. The nuns had trained us for lives as perfect wives, or perfect novitiates in the order. So it was to be God or Man and as I didn't have the makings of a nun I opted for the man and set out to be a good wife. I was twenty-one when I married and still working on the local newspaper, a job to which I proved better suited than domesticity, but I wanted children and

Liz Byrski

believed that eventually I might improve at being a wife. I was wrong about that.

By 1968, when young people around the world were putting their futures and their safety on the line for peace, justice and human rights, I was twenty-four, pregnant with my first child and comfortably uninterested in the maelstrom of political and social protest gripping the world. That summer, as I browsed a stall of battered books at a village jumble sale, I came upon one that looked almost new. I had never heard of the book or its author but at sixpence I thought I could hardly go wrong. It was May Sarton's *Plant Dreaming Deep*, a memoir in which she wrote of her desire for control over her own life, her need for solitude in which to write, her enthusiasm for the adventure of ageing, and of her decision at the age of forty-five to buy a house in a small New Hampshire village, where she could live and write alone. Sarton's passion and intensity, her fierce honesty about women's emotional reality, about solitude and ageing, both thrilled and shocked me. I was reading the raw and moving inner life of a much older woman on a distant continent, but she articulated so much of what I felt. I had no idea then that I was

44

immersed in the work of a feminist writer. I don't think I'd even heard of feminism then, but I was nursing my aspirations to become a writer. Five years after *Plant Dreaming Deep*, I read Sarton's *Journal of a Solitude* in which she wrote with passionate intensity of the anger forbidden to women and the frequent conflicts between the emotional work of being a woman and the writer's need for solitude.

Perhaps my solitary nature, combined with the polite hostility of my parents' marriage was not the best preparation for my own marriage. I had developed a strong and independent inner life and resented the expectation that this would take second place to domesticity. So Sarton's writing hit the spot. Even so I had always wanted children and for seven years I tried hard to make the marriage work. By that time we had two sons and I realised that I could enjoy and care for children in a way that I could not enjoy or adjust to marriage. I left home with a four-year-old and a four month-old baby. Some years later I married and failed again, this time after twelve years and for much the same reasons. But by that time the women's movement had enabled me to name my discontents and I attempted to negotiate for a change in the relationship, but negotiation and change were not even up for discussion. I left home again. On both occasions it was scary and I had no real idea how I would cope in practical or financial terms, so my sons, now in their forties, are testament to my great good fortune and the fact that there were at least a few things I must have got right.

Through my thirties and forties old age, and the rewards and freedoms that it represented, seemed a long way off as I juggled being wife, mother and sole parent, always with a full-time job or a freelance business. There was little time for contemplation or for writing anything that wasn't going to produce enough to pay the bills. In 1981 my second husband was offered a job in Perth and once we had found a place to live and my sons were settled in school I set myself up as a freelance journalist and spent my days, and frequently my nights, searching out stories and commissions which would pay the bills, attempting to negotiate deadlines and, once having delivered the work, surviving the anxious wait to get paid before the next bills came in. Future planning was short term and designed to keep the wolf from the door. My husband had quit the job that brought us to Australia and for several years I was the sole breadwinner. In the late eighties, I accepted a permanent full-time job as a producer and broadcaster with ABC Radio in Perth. Live radio, with its voracious appetite for stories, interviews, celebrity guests and talkback topics, is an exhausting daily roller-coaster of very short deadlines in which tomorrow's schedule is a yawning black hole that drains energy and creativity. For most of those years I saw the world through the lens of the five or ten minute interview or the thirty-second grab. From radio I moved to the tense and overheated environment of the office of a minister in the state government and then back again to radio. But as I reached my fifties, twice divorced and living alone, ageing was becoming a reality; this was my time and I was determined to get it right.

I began to fill a notebook with fragments of my desires and aims for old age, along with clippings, pictures and quotes to help me create a picture of the life I wanted and the sort of old person I wanted to be. There were plans for writing, travel, yoga, treks across Europe and India, learning to weave, singing lessons, joining a choir, piano lessons. There were questions of faith and ethics, ideas about how to live both well and productively and to contribute something of value. I wish I could say that I took those jottings, mapped them out and then followed the plan, but of course I didn't, realising the contents of that notebook would occupy several lifetimes. Where to start? What did I care most about? What did I *really* believe in? How did trekking around the world fit with the need for a settled life with long periods in which to write and read? Should I plan for the long term or approach life one day at a time? And which of the ingredients in this melting pot of feelings, thoughts, ideas, plans and goals did I really passionately want, and which had I added because it seemed cool or fashionable? The notebook freaked me out. Each time I glanced at it my heart rate increased and I searched the fridge for chocolate. I had created a monster and early one morning, as the notebook hovered distractingly on the periphery of my vision, I grabbed it, raced out to the pavement and dropped it in the bin as the garbage truck trundled towards the gate. Things got better after that.

In the weeks that followed some guiding themes began to emerge: a desire to live more fully in the moment, to be kinder to others and to myself, to grow in knowledge, wisdom, confidence and peace of mind and banish the unfocused, low-level anxiety that had become my constant companion. Changing oneself is never easy and the road to the good life of ageing is not only paved with good intentions but scattered with the potholes of a dominant culture in which age is something to be reviled, disguised and avoided for as long as possible.

And then, in my late fifties, happily resigned to living alone, fate and romance wrenched me out of the emotional safety of my solitude and back into the turmoil of a relationship. I was on holiday in England and went to stay with Irene, a friend who lived in the house next door to my parents' old home. When I arrived Irene gave me a letter; someone had been looking for me, and had traced me to Australia. He had tried to call me there, but I had been in Portugal visiting my son and my house sitter had given him Irene's address and phone number. He had called her, then sent this letter in time for my arrival and would call again that evening. As I ripped open the envelope and read the letter I had had no idea I was about to embark on a life-changing experience that would drag me to the heights of romantic love and the depths of despair and disappointment, and would eventually enable me to define how I wanted to live.

The letter came from the man I had fallen in love with in 1961 at the age of seventeen. He was German, divorced and living in America but working temporarily in London; it was romantic, passionate and doomed. Six months later, when he had to go home to San Francisco he asked me to marry him and my parents, who liked him but thought him entirely unsuitable for me, said no. But they did agree that if, in a year's time, we still wanted to marry they would give their permission. He left and I was bereft. For several months we wrote several times a week and then suddenly, and without my really understanding why, he ended it and I really was brokenhearted. I didn't hear from him again until the day I opened that letter 37 years later, and spoke to him on the telephone later that evening.

'I made a terrible mistake,' he told me. 'You were ... you always have been, the love of my life.'

Across the decades and continents and despite it being a time when I was committed to the single life, the chance to try again was too strong to resist. How many of us are given the opportunity to pursue in later life the love that was lost in youth? Three weeks later, after daily transatlantic telephone calls, we met in Frankfurt and spent two weeks together.

Perhaps the most extraordinary feature of this late-life romantic adventure is the way that at this point our individual narratives of the past instantly merged and then, in the ensuing months, slowly began to unravel under the pressure of reality. To be chased halfway around the world by the one that got away was wildly exciting and seductive. I put my Australian life on hold and moved to California. I stayed there for almost a year but I should have left much earlier because it soon became clear that he really was looking for the girl he left behind – a girl who was submissive, passive, never argued with him, had few opinions of her own and was, best of all, slim. For a while I convinced myself that I could be and wanted to be that girl again. On reflection this astounds me as I had spent decades trying to become a very different person from the one I had been in youth. But I entered into his fantasy and made it my own. I allowed it to undermine me to a surprising degree before my true adult self broke through to rescue me. I had struggled far too long with the awkward dissonance of being loved for the girl I used to be rather than the woman I had become: mid-fifties, fiercely independent, with strong opinions that differed widely from his, ready to challenge his authority at every turn, and no longer slim.

Leaving this relationship, which my friends and family had observed with surprise and concern, was long and painful. I already had a strong sense of shame at my inability to build a lasting relationship and now I had failed again. As I recovered I came to understand that through the hurt and the humiliation of recognising that in my late fifties I was living out someone else's fantasy, I had learned a great deal about myself. I understood the strength of that part of myself that needs space for an inner life, needs that to be respected and resists intrusion.

According to the late writer Carolyn Heilbrun, 'It is perhaps only in old age, certainly past fifty, that women can stop being female impersonators, and can grasp the opportunity to reverse their most cherished

principles of "femininity."' In all my relationships I had tried to play the role for
which my family, my schooling and the social climate in which I grew up had prepared
me. It was a role in which I was destined to
fail because it required me to be other than
myself. I felt terrible shame at this attempt to
be the girl that was left behind but it helped
me to put my past in perspective and shaped
how I now face old age.

I was determined that this was the end
of love. I said 'never again' many times and
really meant it. But then, at sixty-three, I
met a truly evolved man, firmly grounded
in reality. One who, while more outgoing
than me, has a need for intellectual and creative space, similar to my own. And so I fell
in love again, this time with someone who
can see and understand who I am and ac-
tually likes that. In age I can relish for the
first time, the freedom to be myself within a
relationship; to be liberated from tradition-
al expectations and loved for and in spite of
my difference.

When I was filling that scary notebook
with ideas and plans for the future I as-
sumed that travel would be an important
element of my old age. I saw myself ageing
in comfortable old clothes with a backpack,

sitting in a café in Vienna with my laptop, or with a notebook beside me in a restaurant in Budapest, walking through showers of russet autumn leaves in Boston, in India gazing at the wonders of the Taj Mahal or rapt in the treasures of the Uffizi in Florence. But in the last couple of years I have had to acknowledge that the peripatetic life doesn't suit me. I don't travel well or comfortably. I don't adapt easily to working in different places, and distance and disruption create anxiety. I am at my best at home, surrounded by the familiarity of my favourite things, particularly my books and the bits of technology that keep me in touch with the world. To be heading towards seventy with the prospect of continuing to do what I most enjoy is a privilege. For me, knowing that I am not alone is the bedrock of the freedom that enables a creative and independent life packed with the love of family and friends, the pleasures and satisfactions of work, and the liberty to greet each day as I choose.

I'm aware that my life would not appeal to many, it doesn't even appeal to many of my own friends, but I suspect there are more people who, as they age, might choose the single life if they had the freedom to do so. In his book *Going Solo: The Extraordinary Rise and Surprising Appeal of Living Alone,* Eric Klinenberg, Professor of Sociology at New York University writes that gerontologists report that older people, particularly older women, express a preference for 'intimacy at a distance', and display no preference for living with a partner or with friends. 'Increasingly, even those single seniors who get involved in romantic relationships prefer "living apart, together"'. Klinenberg explains that the connection to a supportive social network sustains and enables older people to enjoy living alone. 'And this where men's and women's experiences of aging alone differ most sharply, especially after the loss of a spouse. On average women are considerably more skilled at building and sustaining relationships.'

But while older women remain trapped in invisibility there is no need for local, state or federal governments to address questions of how those networks can be facilitated to enable the women, and indeed the men, who make this choice to do so without condemning themselves to loneliness and isolation.

V

On Grief and Regret

> We must come to grief and
> regret anyway – and I for one
> would rather regret the reality
> than its phantasm, knowledge
> than hope, the deed than the
> hesitation, true life and not
> mere sickly potentialities.
> — *A.S. Byatt*

I remember very clearly the moment when
I realised that my relationship with my
parents had changed radically and
forever; the moment when I became the
parent and they the children. It was a
warm spring day in 1994 when they
turned up three-quarters of an hour late
for lunch. My father was a stickler for
punctuality, it was only a fifteen-minute
drive, and I can't recall him ever being late
for anything.

'I've got a very bad feeling about this,' my son Neil said as the car finally pulled into the drive.

As soon as Dad got out of the car it was clear that something was very wrong. At eighty-three he was still a robust man with plenty of energy and an authoritative manner that hadn't changed since he retired twenty years earlier. But today his face was grey and when I took his hands they were icy cold as was his cheek when I kissed him. Over the last year or so he had become forgetful and his driving was somewhat erratic but in every other way he had seemed much as he had always been.

'Your father got lost, several times,' Mum said, tight-lipped.

As they had aged the tension and resentment between them had sharpened. Dad said nothing but he was strangely distracted and didn't seem to understand that they were late. I had set the table for lunch in the garden but despite the warmth of the day he was shivering and Neil fetched him a blanket. It was a strange and awkward meal; Dad rarely spoke and Mum, by then very forgetful and sometimes confused, filled the awkward silences with small talk. It was as we sat with our coffee that my father produced a bulky envelope with a UK stamp.

'It's from Ron. His hands are bad and he can't write much so he's got some stupid idea that we can talk to each other instead.' Dad and Ron had been friends since childhood. Now, on opposite sides of the world, they exchanged long letters once a month. Dad fumbled slightly with the envelope. 'God knows what he's talking about but he sent me this.'

It was a note from Ron suggesting that because his arthritis made it difficult to write they could record their news, and he had enclosed a cassette.

'Well that's a good idea, isn't it?' I asked.

'Ridiculous,' he said, irritable now, waving the cassette. 'What am I supposed to do with this? Never seen anything like it.'

Neil and I exchanged a stunned look across the table. Dad had been using cassettes for years. Neil collected the cassette player from my desk.

'You can play it like you play your other cassettes, Gramps,' he said, slipping it into the machine.

But as Ron's voice boomed out into the garden the fear and confusion on Dad's face made me catch my breath. He was like a

small child caught out in seriously bad behaviour but unsure what he had done
wrong. He had no idea what a cassette was
or how to use it, and he strenuously denied
ever having seen or used one, but his defens-
iveness signalled his fear of finding himself
in a situation he couldn't understand. By
now my mother had decided he was being deliberately bloody minded; there was
a lot of tutting and eye-rolling. Neil and I
tried to steer the conversation in ways that
might jog Dad's memory: the cassettes he
had recorded for me when, in the 1970s,
they lived for several years in Spain, the
cassettes on which Neil had recorded interviews with them both years earlier for a
high school family history project. Nothing
worked, and in that moment it seemed as
though a tiny cigarette burn in his brain had
destroyed everything he had ever known
about cassettes. It was gone, and it was not
coming back. I was now as icy cold as Dad
and blinded with panic about what else may
have been lost and what might happen next.

It comes to many of us and in many different ways but the recognition that the par-
ent/child situation has been reversed is a
brutal one. It's devastating to watch the decline of those you love, especially parents

who are so inevitably a part of who we have become. We spend so much of our lives, consciously or unconsciously, responding to their expectations or rebelling against them and then, one day, their minds and their personalities begin to unravel. Suddenly I was in charge, and each week seemed to bring a new situation that challenged me to question how to balance my belief in their basic right to make decisions about their own lives with the need to care for and manage them, which often meant imposing on them things that were not of their choosing and sometimes against their preference. After three months, endless tests and numerous visits to doctors and specialists, Dad was diagnosed with Alzheimer's disease, and it was made clear to us that a series of small strokes had rapidly exacerbated his condition.

My parents' lives descended into chaos. I had to confiscate Dad's car and, soon after that, he began locking Mum in the house, refusing to allow anyone in, and leaving the gas on and the water running. He had become a danger to himself and to Mum and I had no choice but to remove him from his own home and commit him to residential care against his will. It is, without doubt, the hardest thing I have ever had to do. I felt a lesser person as a result of it and agonised for months over whether I had done the wrong thing when it was, apparently, clear to everyone else that there was no alternative.

Meanwhile my mother became more confused, more forgetful, and her long suppressed anger at my father spilled out. For decades she had relied on him to manage every aspect of their lives; now it was clear that she was frightened. She had always seemed to resent him and now she felt he had abandoned her and she couldn't, or wouldn't, forgive him. Her own dementia meant that she could not understand what had happened, and she refused even to visit him. I took her to live with me, thinking that she would be able to cope with being in the house alone while I was at work, but the dramatic events of the preceding months followed by the move had all done their damage. She wandered around the house getting lost several times a day. 'Help, help,' she would call from a bedroom or the laundry. 'I'm lost, somebody help me.' And while she was always tempted to wander out into the safely walled garden, once there it became a terrifying maze. She was panic-stricken at being left alone and feigned illness every morning when it was time for me to leave for work. There was a day care centre nearby but I knew that it would be anathema to her shyness and solitary nature, and when I organised a carer to come in twice a day, Mum would forget her between each visit. Within a few months she too needed full-time residential care and her hostility to Dad and refusal to have any-thing to do with him meant that I had to find a different location for her. They ended up forty minutes' drive apart, and both as far away again from my home and the ABC studios where I worked. Each evening I left work to visit one or the other before going home, and weekends involved treks to take Mum out to lunch or shopping one day, and Dad the next.

But logistics weren't the only problem. My parents' life crises came at a time when I had a demanding job that I couldn't afford to give up even had I wanted to. It was also a time when, after years of being a sole par-ent, I was relishing the freedom of not being responsible for anyone – not even a dog or a goldfish. So now I had an attitude problem. I really didn't want to be doing this. The parent/child model applied to caring for a parent or parents with Alzheimer's is useful in some respects, but the situation differs in one crucial way. Parenting a child is a process of incremental rewards: the thrill of the first smile, the first tooth, the first steps, the first words, the letters of the alphabet ... small gains that seem dazzling, unique and encouraging steps towards maturity and independence. Caring for a parent with dementia is a journey downward through a series of subtractions – awkward, painful and humiliating, and leading ultimately to loss. Talking to others who have battled resentment at the burden of caring for their aged parents at a time when they were just about to take full advantage of newfound freedom has been a relief. Resenting my parents, who had always loved and tried to do their best for me, is not something I'm proud of; it reveals a dark and selfish aspect of my nature which I'd prefer to hide, but I know I'm not alone in this and perhaps if we can learn to speak more freely about our reactions which feel so shameful, it might be easier to manage them.

Alongside the resentment, I also struggled with the long slow grief of watching Mum and Dad change and decline so that before either of them died they had become people I hardly knew. As I watched them disappearing before my eyes, I hated myself for minding that I was responsible for them. And I recognised too late that by failing to bridge the gaps of their silences and tensions, I had never really understood them. So much was unspoken, so much hidden, that in those final years of both their lives I felt that I had never really gotten to know them nor, as an adult, allowed them to know me. Time does, of course, change everything, and three years after that devastating recognition of role reversal my father died, and three years later my mother was also gone. I was left with a restless conscience, and the recriminations and regret that I could have, should have, managed it all so much better.

Regret, like so much else today, is unfashionable. *Je ne regrette rien* sings the fabulous Edith Piaf in a voice so steeped in regret it gives the lie to her words. I reject the current trend to dismiss regret as useless and self-indulgent and I'm disinclined to believe those who claim they have none, especially in later life. It is from our regrets that we learn so much about ourselves: our strengths and our weaknesses, our faults, our mean-spiritedness, the things that cause us shame and our readiness to compromise our beliefs or values when confronted by the difficulties they can create for us. To cast regret aside seems to me to cast aside the chance to learn and change, and so while regret certainly doesn't rule my life, I'm unwilling to banish it from my mind.

My regrets about my parents are many. Foremost among them is my failure to heed the advice of others about the futility of trying to make a person with dementia understand and accept what is 'real' and 'correct'. I argued too long, too forcefully and too often, particularly with my father. When he told me something outrageous or simply incorrect I insisted on putting him right every time. It was a useless and frustrating exercise and, worse still, I see now that it undermined him at a time when he was most vulnerable. In earlier days I had frequently resented his authority but, even as an adult, rarely summoned the courage to argue with him. But when he was old and sick I argued with him constantly. Now I wonder if this was some sort of revenge in which I needed the triumph of always being right. I always loved him and knew he loved me, and once he was gone I saw how easy it would have been to change the dynamics of that relationship earlier, at a time when we could have met on an equal footing.

I had grown accustomed to the awkwardness of my parents' marriage; so cool and prickly when we were home alone and so perfectly performed to conform to 'normality' in company. Their emotional estrangement was like background music, played low and always slightly off key. Despite that it was a symbiotic relationship and the tyranny of dementia ripped it apart with devastating force. I sense they may have struck a bargain, even before I was born – a bargain, perhaps, about safety, security and convention – that would keep their relationship in apparent shape and ensure its survival. And so my greatest regret is that I didn't try to breach the wall of silence and in turn never confided my own intimate secrets, never disclosed my plans, my failures, my hopes or aspirations, never talked of the times I fell in love and out again, or walked the boundaries of financial disaster. I saw them often and loved them deeply, but we constantly failed to connect. From being at the centre of their lives I moved out to the margins and in doing so I sacrificed the chance to know them better and to let them know me.

The death of my parents left me feeling I had been cut loose. Living on the other side of the world from where I grew up there was no one who had known me as a child. I had an uncle and three cousins in England, but our families had never been close and I hardly knew them. I felt as though my early life had been erased, and the need to revisit the places of childhood became increasingly important. I had lived in Australia for sixteen years before going back to England for a short visit the year my father died, but once they were both gone I needed to connect with the past in other ways and I set out to find my oldest friend.

Evelyn was nine when we first met, I was two years younger, and our situations were dramatically different. We lived in a beautiful old wattle and daub cottage with white walls, black beams, a stable door, and diamond-paned leadlight windows, standing in five acres of its own land. I went to a small convent, and in the fifties we had holidays in France and Spain, when most of the other girls at school were holidaying in Cornwall, Devon or the Channel Islands.

Evelyn's parents had a very small farm: one cow, half a dozen pigs, some chickens, geese and ducks. It was barely more than subsistence and the family's only other source of income came from casual work: her mother cleaned houses, her father cut hedges and trimmed verges. But the difference in our situations seemed not to matter. I found the privations of Evelyn's home mysterious and exciting while she found the comparative luxury of mine an endless source of pleasure.

While I had small household chores to do before I could go out to play, Evelyn had serious responsibilities on the farm and in the house, scrubbing floors, washing laundry, cleaning out the pigsty and the chicken house, and much more. So our time together was always limited, but as we became older and long afternoons and summer evenings stretched ahead of us, we grew closer. We would lie talking at the shady heart of a huge rhododendron bush, take long treks through the woods to a nearby lake, bash a ball around with two old tennis racquets, or take the bus to the swimming pool for the afternoon, stopping on our way back to buy threepence worth of chips to eat on the bus home.

Our friendship survived in a more limited way once Evelyn left school, got a job and a year later left home, and then I did the same, but it lasted until the year we both got married. But when Evelyn and her new husband moved away from the area the distance meant that we drifted apart. That was 1965, and it was 2001 before I set out to find her again, through the Friends Reunited website.. Four weeks later my email had gone unanswered and I had come to the conclusion that she had decided not to respond, and then, in that same week, a message arrived. She had had to think seriously, she said, about whether she wanted to be drawn back into what had been a truly horrible childhood, but she had decided to take the risk. She was planning a holiday in Australia later that year with a friend and in her third email she told me that she had reorganised their itinerary to include a few days in Perth.

Seven months later we met in the foyer of the Perth Sheraton. Evelyn seemed unchanged – I would have recognised her anywhere – and she said the same of me. We went out to dinner and sat at the table for more than four hours until the staff asked us to leave so they could close the restaurant. That night Evelyn told me that by breathing life back into our friendship I had helped her to remember that in a miserable, poverty-stricken childhood riven with violence there had also been times of pure and unadulterated happiness. I told her that she had given me back my own childhood, validated it and enriched it in a way no one else could have done. The following year I went to England and Evelyn met me at the airport driving the latest model gold BMW convertible. We screeched with laughter over the fact that she was now a very wealthy woman driving a huge, expensive and flashy car, while I was endeavouring to keep my head above water as a writer and drove a ten-year-old Corolla.

Over the next few years we emailed regularly, talked on the phone, and met several more times in England. I stayed with Evelyn for the last time in late 2009, and the day before I was due to leave I walked into her kitchen to find her standing white and rigid by the telephone. She had just taken a call from the hospital; tests conducted the previous week showed that she had cancer in her liver and lungs and a prognosis that the coming Christmas would be her last. But thanks to her incredible spirit and determination she lived through that Christmas and the next. Her emails and phone calls were full of news about how well she was doing and full of her determination to survive. Then, eighteen months after the diagnosis, my phone rang at two in the morning and suddenly, shockingly, she was gone.

It was so sudden and shocking that it didn't seem real and perhaps the fact that the news came in the early hours of the morning added to that sense of unreality. But with daylight came the realisation that for months I had allowed myself to believe that she had stopped dying, that her incredible determination was enough to stop the cancer cells multiplying and wreaking havoc in her body. For me at least she performed wellness, even signs of recovery, and I was convinced because I wanted to be.

Surely one of the hardest parts of ageing is the loss of those we love, and the deepened understanding of our own mortality that their passing brings. Those odd and inexplicable pains that strike in the night, a rash, a tightness in the chest that might be indigestion or something more sinister, all acquire significance as we age and as we lose those of our own age or younger. I wonder where I have put my will, what sort of funeral I want, and then another hour or another day goes by and life stretches out again. Less than a century ago death was so much more a part of life than it is today. Children watched as their grandparents, their parents and frequently their siblings died in their own homes; the reality of death was all around. Today we have separated death from life, hiding it from children for as long as we can, sanitising it and shrouding it in fear and mystery, pretending it's not going to happen and so it is usually shocking, unexpected and unbelievable; confusing and frightening for children and, for the elderly, deeply and uncomfortably personal.

I grieve still for my parents and for my dear and oldest friend. That grief and the regrets about what I got wrong, what I missed, wasted or neglected during the course of their lives reinforces the uniqueness of what they brought to mine. It is that mature mix of grief and regret that brings to ageing a tender melancholy that adds richness and texture to my life.

VI

Family and Friends

> I like the word affection because it signifies something habitual.
> — *Mary Wollstonecraft*

I began writing this section on a hot summer afternoon in Perth and wrote only two paragraphs before a ringtone reminded me that I had lost track of time. At four o'clock on Saturdays I have a date with my grandsons on Skype. For the last ten years, Sam and Jamie have lived with their mother in England. The twins were four years old when my son and his wife separated and this year they will be fifteen. Maintaining a relationship at such a distance has not been easy, especially when they were younger. Each spaced-out visit involved getting to know each other anew, and telephone conversations were more like interviews. But as all three of us have grown older, more frequent visits have helped us to establish more points of connection and now technology enables us to see each other as well as to talk. I'm introduced to the two new cats who are brought unwillingly to the computer and create havoc by leaping onto the keyboard. Jamie plays the latest tune he has learned on his ukulele; Sam shows me the Eccles cakes he made at school. There is continuity and connection. I admire their t-shirts or new haircuts, relate embarrassing anecdotes about their father and uncle, and take them on a virtual tour of my home with the iPad. It's not what I expected of grandparenting but it's a whole lot better than it would have been without technology.

If I flick across to Facebook I can see a photograph of Mark, their father, and his wife, Sarah, taken yesterday in Sydney, and another of Neil and his partner, Bill, on holiday and shopping for books in Melbourne, and then there's another of my 21-year-old step-granddaughter, Ashley, who is recovering from meningitis. I could Skype all of them now and have them live on my screen in minutes. When I rage against the tyranny of technology, its capacity to dehumanise us, occupy hours of precious time and generate infuriating telephone conversations with technical support, I try to remember that as I age it is technology that will allow me to see and speak to friends and family as often as I wish. I'm among the first generation of parents and grandparents for whom all this is a possibility.

Years ago I heard someone say, 'A mother can only ever be as happy as her unhappiest child.' I understood the veracity of this as my sons grew from childhood, through their teens and into adulthood. I wondered if there would ever be a time when their periods of happiness would coincide. They did, they do now, and so I am counting my (and their) blessings. Is the reality of loving someone more than you love yourself, of knowing that you would take their physical and emotional pain for them if you could, that you would push them into the last two seats in the lifeboat, or step back into the burning building to rescue them, unique to parenthood?

As an ageing parent my greatest joy and satisfaction is the love and friendship of my adult children. I struggle to suppress the instinctive 'mother' type questions and responses but frequently slip up. I still manage to interfere, provide unwanted advice and express anxiety, and they manage to ignore it. But increasingly my sons are not only my friends, they are also the people to whom I turn for advice, or to sound out an idea on anything from moving house to upgrading my computer, from where to find the best airfares to how to organise my old age. As we negotiate the various shifts in the mother/son relationship I'm hoping there will be plenty more time before they face the dramatic final confrontation of role reversal. 'Live long enough to embarrass and annoy your children,' the saying goes, and I'm already doing that. Despite my hit and miss parenting, they have become wise, loving and intelligent men of whom I am enormously proud, and now their partners have also become my friends and family. I wish it hadn't taken me so many years to learn that reading them stories, having conversations and adventures and simply hanging out with them was more important to all of us than ironing their pyjamas or vacuuming their rooms. But together we survived their childhood and they have emerged triumphant. What more could any parent ask?

It was the anthropologist Margaret Mead who coined the phrase 'post-menopausal zest' to describe the energetic social and companionate lives of older women, and it is undoubtedly true that as women age we tend to turn more to the company of other women. Retaining heterosexual relationships or finding new ones in later life is still important for many ageing women, as are supportive friendships with men. But once past mid-life and menopause many women's immersion in heterosexual reality lessens and their pursuit of relationships in later life seems to lack the edge of neediness many men demonstrate as they age without a partner. Many women who have spent decades relating to and taking care of men and children find a new kind of freedom as they explore the possibilities of the friendship and companionship of other women. And women who have always defined themselves as heterosexual may embark for the first time on a same-sex relationship, finding the comfort and mutual loving care that they relish in old age.

'You have to give up your friendships when you marry,' my mother had told me before I married. 'Husbands don't want women friends hanging around.' Was this a social convention, something that her own mother had told her, or was it personal experience? The latter seems unlikely as my father, although something of an introvert, was very much at ease in the company of women, and they liked and, I believe, trusted him. Whatever the reality, the sacrifice of her women friends was something Mum had taken seriously. My parents' relationship always lacked a sense of companionship and my father was often away from home on business, but Mum didn't compensate for this by developing friendships with women, even in later life. Perhaps by then her 'aloneness' had become a habit. The absence of women in her life struck me most profoundly at her funeral when the only women present were my friends who were there for me. When my parents got engaged in 1932, Mum gave up her life as a dancer and teacher of dancing, to help Dad run his electrical engineering business. They married in 1939, the week before war was declared, I was born five years later and soon after that the business was sold and Dad joined Marks & Spencer where he rapidly moved into the higher levels of the executive hierarchy. They had friendships with other couples both then and until Dad retired, and when they moved to Spain and then here to Australia. When I reflect on

Mum's life, that absence of friendships with women seems extraordinarily sad.

For centuries women were confined to marriages, domestic arrangements and work situations that separated and often alienated them from other women. 'The friendships of men have enjoyed glory and acclamation, but the friendships of women have not been merely unsung but mocked, belittled and falsely interpreted,' Vera Brittain wrote in 1947. But the women's movement changed that by celebrating women's friendship and demonstrating what can happen when women work together for a collective goal.

All women, whether they define themselves as feminist or not, have benefited from the changes of the seventies and eighties, and from the liberation of women's friendships that came with the women's movement. And in writing fiction about older women I have wanted to celebrate the sort of friendships with women that have been so precious for me, particularly since my late thirties when I first came to live in Australia. When I'm speaking to groups of women the value of their friendships is always a part of the conversation. It keeps them sane, they say, enables them to let off

steam without having to negotiate the sens-
itivities of partners and children. And then
there is the fun, the laughter, the mutual
understandings and the unspoken but profoundly felt sense that these are the people
to whom one will turn during the worst
and the best of times. But perhaps most of
all it is the sheer pleasure of being understood, of linking into the consciousness of
being female in what is still a predominantly
male-ordained world.

'Perhaps being old is having lighted
rooms /Inside your head, and people in
them, acting.' Perhaps it is – but I've also
wondered whether, in this line of his poem
'The Old Fools', Phillip Larkin was also
speaking about being a writer. If I exchange
'old' for 'a writer' it seems to describe the
process of writing fiction, of living in close
company for months on end with a set of
characters to whom one has responsibilities.
When the characters don't behave as one
wants them to, when they refuse to work together, and get in each other's way, sorting
them out and trying to get them to their final destination seems horribly burdensome
and frustrating. 'I love the characters, they
really become my friends,' readers often tell
me. 'I wish you'd write a sequel.' But I

doubt I ever will because by the time I've finished a book I am heartily glad to get those characters out of my head. But the lighted rooms of old age are a very appealing prospect.

Over time some friendships fade away, either from our personal choice or on their own, and I believe that as one ages the circle of friendship begins to draw in. By a slow process of cultivation we cherish some more than others, feed and nurture those friendships while others lie fallow. We learn which friendships nourish us and which drain us. And what we are left with then are a chosen few whom we know and trust, people whom we love and who will love and tolerate us at the times when we are least attractive and most needy, who will both grieve and celebrate with us. For me these are some very special women, and some wise and generous men, who still tolerate, even seem fond of, my strange habits and strong views, who make me laugh and, sometimes, cry, and who I hope will inhabit the lighted rooms in my head when I am very old.

VII

Whatever Next?

> Not knowing when the dawn will come I open every door.
>
> — *Emily Dickinson*

Three days, three months, three years or thirty – maybe more, none of us knows how long we have left, but the sense of time running out becomes stronger past sixty and much stronger still, I find, since sixty-five. 'You're just a beginner, darl,' a 92-year old woman told me recently, from the seat of the tractor she's still driving. 'Every year it gets even better and you'll find you get better at it.' I believe her. I have great expectations for the future.

Apart from those odd flashes about mortality I don't think much about dying, I certainly don't dwell on it. But as each year passes the need to cram more into the time I have left gathers urgency; I push against the fear of time running out before I have done all that I want to do. But that wanting is not about a specific goal or goals, it isn't about ambition, worldly success or money, it is just about wanting more time with what I've already got, longer to do more of what I'm doing, more time to be with family and friends and more time to learn more about everything that fascinates me. I've met and sometimes interviewed people my age and older who can be quite specific about things they want to experience and achieve before they die. 'After that I'll be happy to go,' they say. I can't imagine feeling like that but perhaps it is a feeling that comes later in age, because right now I feel I never want to let go. I have waited a long time for the satisfaction of being an old woman and I'm determined to enjoy it.

I do dwell often, however, on the fear of losing my independence and mobility. I try to think ahead about managing that and sometimes become concerned about small things I should do to make my house more age friendly, easier to use with a loss of physical strength, free of hazards such as small steps between rooms on which I might trip, and storage cupboards that are too high to reach without a stepladder. Last week I dropped an earring and it bounced away and rolled under the bed. Getting down on the floor now seems a bit of a drama, so once there I lay on the floor remembering how easy it once was to get up and down; how as a child one falls easily and bounces back and how much movement we take for granted throughout most of our lives. Then I rolled over on my side to look under the bed for my earring, but I had left my glasses on the dressing table and couldn't see a thing, I couldn't even see if there was anything else I could do while I was down there, so I concentrated instead on the operation of getting up again.

From the age of four until sixteen I was educated in a convent and there I learned to value faith, and to totally distrust the church and organised religion. Over the years the nature of my faith has changed in many ways but it has always been and still is a life support and an inspiration. For me it is essential to believe not only in something greater than myself but also greater than human beings. I want to believe that there is more than this – and my spiritual life informs my present and my future and influences my approach to ageing and to death.

I think back often to the way I watched the old people who filled my childhood and feel I owe them a debt of gratitude for making old age look inviting rather than something to fear and fight. May Sarton rejoiced in the reality of her ageing – she had looked forward to it, longed for it and was always determined to explore its possibilities and meet its challenges with a steely eye and rigorous enquiry. 'Old age,' she wrote at seventy, 'is life enhancing', and the joys of life have nothing to do with staying young but in enjoying and valuing each stage of life. 'Now I wear the inside person outside and am more comfortable with myself. In some ways I am younger because I can admit vulnerability and more innocent because I do not have to pretend.' She believed one should always live as though one were dying because it brings the priorities into sharp relief. She wrote that she could cope with life so much better at seventy than at fifty, 'partly because I have learned to glide instead of to force myself at moments of tension'.

So now I am learning to glide – to let go of tensions, to remember that I have nothing to prove and need no one's approval but my own. I frequently fall off the glider and struggle to regain my position, but I'm getting better at it.

And so it seems to me a small tragedy that in the second decade of the twenty-first century, as more of us than in any previous time head into an old age that will be longer and could be richer and more fulfilling than that of any previous generation, so much time and energy is spent on a market-driven fight against ageing, and on reciting the hardships and deprivations of old age. And so much anger drives the public conversation about the deleterious effects and financial burden of an ageing population. I want instead a positive conversation in which the phrase 'the fight against ageing' is banned and the use of 'anti-ageing' as a descriptor for any product is greeted with derision. I long for a conversation in which the faces and voices of older people have equal exposure with those of the middle-aged and young; in which the stories of older people are listened to, produced and distributed in a variety of intelligent, respectful and entertaining cultural forms, and in which the experience and wisdom of the elderly is valued and used to inform the future. And most of all I want to see the social contract honoured for the people who struggled hard through difficult times. I want a government that fosters respect and understanding and has the wisdom and the courage to embrace the challenge of implementing the policies that will foster the development of social networks, and deliver high-quality services for care in the community. A government that has the courage to look at the scale and value of the unpaid work of older women, and face the challenge of providing ways of relieving some of it and supporting those who want to continue with it.

And most of all I want to dispel the elitism of youth and even middle age that creates a sort of blindness about old people. I want to ask these younger generations to stop turning away and start looking, and not just looking but *seeing* old people and thinking about who they are and who and what that may have been. To put aside the blinding fear of age and think instead about the richness and the value of lives that have been and still are being lived. Yes – I want a lot and I want it now.

I have planned for my own old age – not in all the ways I should have done by making adequate financial provision, by getting all my papers in order, or stocking up on incontinence pads. I have planned for enjoyment, new adventures and satisfaction. I have planned for and visualised the pleasures of work, of leisure, of solitude, passion, love and adventure as an old woman, not as some lesser sort of woman. My face and body bear no resemblance to the airbrushed perfection of glamour for the ageing woman. But this is *my* face, lined and with broken veins and age spots, and this is *my* body which, for all the unwanted kilos and saggy bits, has served me long and well. My life is in my face and I am happy to live within it.

An enthusiasm for ageing is anyone's for the taking. In May Sarton's journals women discovered the prospects of a vibrant, often turbulent, but always interesting and satisfying old age, the joys of solitude and simple pleasures. But a cultural obsession with youth sustained by the fear and loathing of old age deprives the young and the middle-aged of images of who and what they might become. It limits the imagination of what old age can be and how it might be enjoyed.

For much of my life I have wished I could channel May Sarton. Her insight into the contradictions and conflicting demands of being a woman and a writer, the challenges of solitude and most particularly of ageing, have helped me to understand myself. For years I put off reading Margot Peters's 1998 biography for fear that I might not find within it the woman whose work inspired and comforted me, but eventually I succumbed. I discovered some things I really did not anticipate, some black holes that those journals concealed. But the conflicted character they reveal is even more endearing in her flawed humanity. Sarton's gift to me and to the millions of other women who have devoured her journals is an enthusiasm for and curiosity about growing old which makes me value each day. I strive to pass on that gift and, from time to time, I encounter younger people who are brave enough and open minded enough to consider it.

Acknowledgements

I'm delighted to have been given the opportunity of making my first foray into the brave new world of digital publishing by the very cool and dynamic team at Momentum Books. Joel Naoum and Mark Harding have been endlessly patient in their efforts to drag me into the second decade of the 21st century. It's been a big learning curve, and I'm very grateful.

My thanks also to Cate Paterson, my publisher at Pan Macmillan, for urging me into new waters, and to editor Jo Jarrah for her forensic eye for detail combined with her insight on broader issues.

Thanks too to Graham Murdock for pulling me back from excessive self-indulgence after reading the first draft.

References

I: Women and the Double Standard of
   Ageing

'The double standard about aging': Sontag,
   Susan. 'The Double Standard of
   Aging.' *Saturday Review* 55 (1972).
   Reprinted in Pearsall, Marilyn. *The
   Other Within Us: Feminist Explora-
   tions of Women and Aging*, Colorado:
   West View Press 1997.

'the way this society limits how women': Ibid

'a class struggle, which, like race and
   gender, becomes a filter': de Beauvoir,
   Simone. *On Age*. Middlesex: Penguin
   Books, 1970.

'For most women aging means': Sontag. 'The Double Standard of Aging.'

'The flattered self is a mediated self,': de Zengotita, Thomas. *Mediated: How the Media Shape Your World*. London: Bloomsbury, 2005.

II: Invisible Women

'If we do not know what we are going to be': de Beauvoir, Simone. *The Coming of Age*. New York: G.B. Putnam's Sons, 1972.

III: The Personal Is Political

'If we continue to see our own age through the eyes of observers': Greer, Germaine. 'Serenity and Power.' In Pearsall, Marilyn. *The Other Within Us: Feminist Explorations of Women and Aging*. Colorado: West View Press, 1997.

'attempts to elasticise one's real age': Jones, Meredith. *Skintight: An Anatomy of Cosmetic Surgery*. Oxford: 2008.

IV: Facing Age

'I have always longed to be old': Sarton, May. *At Seventy.* New York: Norton, 1984.

'But I entered into his fantasy and made it my own': Byrski, Liz. *Remember Me.* Fremantle: Fremantle Press, 2000.

'It is perhaps only in old age': Heilbrun, Carolyn. *Writing a Woman's Life.* New York: Ballantine Books, 1988.

'And this where men's and women's experiences of aging': Klinenburg, Eric. *Going Solo: The Extraordinary Rise and Surprising Appeal of Living Alone.* New York: Penguin, 2012.

V: On Grief and Regret

'We must come to grief and regret': Byatt, A.S. *Possession.* London: Knopf Doubleday , 1991.

VI: Family and Friends

'I like the word affection': Wollstonecraft, Mary. Ed. Ingpen, Roger. *The Love Letters of Mary Wollstonecraft to Gilbert Imlay. London: Hutchinson & Co., 1908.*

'Perhaps being old is having lighted rooms': Larkin, Philip. The Old Fools. *Collected Poems.* London Faber and Faber

VII: Whatever Next?

'Not knowing when the dawn will come': Dickinson, Emily. 'Part Two: Nature.' The Complete Poems of Emily Dickinson. Boston: Little Brown, 1924.

'partly because I have learned to glide': Sarton, May. *At Seventy.*

Printed in Australia
AUOC02n1056030614
261470AU00001B/1/P